St. N

St. Nicholas

Told by
Jakob Streit

with
Illustrations by
Georges A. Feldmann

Translated by
Monica Gold

MERCURY PRESS

With permission from the publisher of the original
German *Geschichten vom Schenken und Helfen des
Sankt Nikolaus,* Verlag Freies Geistesleben,
2. Auflage 1990

Cover with a watercolor by Georges A. Feldmann

Printed and published in the USA
Mercury Press
Fellowship Community
241 Hungry Hollow Road
Spring Valley, New York 10977

Contents

St. Nicholas

Nowadays Saint Nicholas appears only at Christmas time and he almost always wears a red coat. But there are also times when he comes in a fur coat or in a dark cloak. Perhaps there are many people who come in the name of St. Nicholas, but only very few are genuine and many are false. How can one distinguish between them? In order to answer that question we begin by telling why there is a St. Nicholas. We will hear the story of the very first St. Nicholas, who really did exist.

St. Nicholas, the Boy

It all began in the city of Patera in Asia Minor where a little boy was born to Johanna and Epiphanius. They named him Nicholas. As he was their first and only child, they gave him all the love and attention that parents can give. Later the family moved to Myra, a city close to the sea. There they lived in a beautiful house, because the father was a rich merchant.

One day when Nicholas was old enough to crawl, his mother was bathing him in a wooden tub. He was so happy to be in the warm water that he suddenly stood up and with both hands splashed water all over his mother while screaming with delight and joy at his ability to share all this water with her. Her dress became totally soaked, so she had to call his father to come and lift the boy out of the bathtub. When the father appeared, he was

greeted by a resounding splash and soon his face too was dripping with water, while Nicholas was screeching with delight. This was the first gift that Nicholas gave: bath-water!

When Nicholas was a few years older, he loved to play with little white stones and pebbles that he collected everywhere. With these stones he created pictures and patterns in the yard in front of his house. Other children joined him and he was always very happy to share and to have them play with him, for together they had more fun.

They laid out stone circles and created sharp-edged figures.

One day, from the poor part of the city, there came a young boy whom the locals called "Pico the rascal." On several occasions he had stolen things in the neighborhood and had been caught. When he stood close to Nicholas and his playmates and saw that there was nothing to take away from them, he grabbed a broom and destroyed the figures that the children had laid on the ground. With all his strength he threw the broom on the ground. It's handle struck Nicholas hard in the head. Pico grinned and skipped away. Nicholas hurried crying to his mother. She comforted him, cooled the wound, placed a healing herb on it, and bandaged his head.

Nicholas asked: "Mother, why has Pico destroyed everything?" His mother answered: "You know, Nicholas, Pico is a boy whose parents are poor and they live in the poorest part of the city. Often they have little food and nobody loves Pico."

When Nicholas looked out of the window with his mother, he saw that the other children were actively collecting the scattered stones. Some had already begun to repair the damaged figures. "Look," said his mother, "one can repair everything." She gave Nicholas a large orange. "I will go and help," Nicholas said. His mother nodded.

Nicholas hurried down the steps. When he reached the front of the house, he stood there for a moment. Suddenly he turned and ran toward the poor part of the city.

Everywhere he asked people: "Where does Pico live, where does Pico live?" until someone showed him a small, simple hut. It had only one door and a window. Nicholas knocked. Pico opened. For a moment he stared at Nicholas with his bandaged head, then slammed the door in Nicholas' face.

Inside, Nicholas heard loud words. Undecided about what to do, he simply remained standing. Then the door opened again. A woman asked in a gruff manner: "What do you want?" Nicholas replied: "Here, I want to give this orange to Pico, and to ask him if he wants to play with me." Pico's mother shook her head, mumbled a little, then grumbled: "Come in!" Nicholas stepped into the dusky, dark kitchen. On the glowing fire there stood a three-legged pan with a brown, watery soup. Pico sat next to it looking gloomy.

"Here, Pico," said Nicholas "I wanted to bring you this orange, because nobody loves you." The mother's jaw dropped, and Pico cast an uncertain glance at Nicholas and at the magnificent orange. At that time of year oranges were scarce.

Nicholas walked to the boy and placed the orange in his hand, saying: "Pico, come and visit me; I would like to play with you!" After speaking these words and now feeling quite sick, he disappeared through the door; he found it just too difficult to breathe in that smelly kitchen.

That evening Nicholas' mother put him to bed. He recited his evening prayer. His mother had removed the bandage for the night, for she could see that the big lump on his forehead was almost healed. Suddenly Nicholas said: "Mother, today I went to the poor part of the city. I found Pico and gave him the orange because nobody loves him. And in the kitchen there was a terrible smell of boiling soup. I told him he should come and play with me."

Astonished, yes, even shocked, his mother Johanna looked at him: "Nicholas, why did you go to the poor part of the city without telling me?" Nicholas pointed to his heart and answered: "In here something moved me to go."

Just at that moment his father Epiphanius entered the room to say good night to his boy. His wife told him what had happened. Epiphanius read the Bible every day and thought of the words: "Do good to those who hate you," and then was silent for a while. Nicholas asked him: "Pico may play with me, right father? Together we can create figures with the little stones, feed the fish, heat the baking oven, carry water. There is so much to be done, and it is much more fun to do it together." "We will see," said his father Epiphanius. "Good night, Nicholas!" He kissed his boy on the forehead, quite close to the bump, and left the room. In the evening the parents spoke for a long time about Nicholas. They decided to try it with Pico, so that he would have a playmate. Yet they decided to wait to see whether Pico would come by himself, and they explained to Nicholas that no one should go to fetch him.

Will Pico Come?

Two days passed. Again and again Nicholas ran to the window, wondering whether Pico would come. On the third morning he fixed his gaze on a place a short distance from his home. There was a well to which women came to wash their clothes. As Nicholas strained his eyes to see who all was there, he discovered a young boy with black hair who sat there on a stone cleaning his feet.

Wasn't that Pico? Now he got up and washed his head and hair. From time to time he looked over at Nicholas' house. Then he took something out of his pants pocket and washed it in the well. He kept this thing in his hand. Again he looked across at the house. Then he ventured a few hesitant steps. He came closer and closer. Now he had seen Nicholas looking out of the upper window. He turned around and stood still. Then a clear voice called out: "Picooo!" and the boy approached the house.

Nicholas ran down the steps. When he opened the door, Pico stood there with cleanly washed, bare feet. In his outstretched hand he held a shining seashell: "For you, Nicholas! My father gave it to me. He found it on the seashore."

Nicholas and Pico became good friends. Mother Johanna gave him gifts of clothes and shoes. Once Nicholas asked Pico: "What does your father do for work?" Pico responded: "Dead, drowned. Ship sank." From then on Nicholas loved him even more.

The Little Cart

Nicholas' father was a merchant and often away on trips. He owned two ships. One carried corn, the other salt, and they sailed all the way across the ocean. Once he went to a carriage builder and asked him to connect four little wheels to axles. He went to Nicholas and Pico and said to them: "Now you can build a cart for yourselves and with it you can shop for your mother in the city. Go to the shed. There you will find tools and plenty of wood." Now there was much work for the two boys to do. When they had problems, they went to the carriage builder and asked him for advice. The finished cart was wonderful to play with.

At that time there was a depression in the land. A bad harvest had brought in very little grain for the farmers. Father Epiphanius had large storage elevators filled with the grain that he had ordered from across the sea.

In the poor part of the city there lived many very poor people who had nothing to eat. Nicholas asked his mother: "May we give some of our large supply of grain to the poor? When father comes home his ships will bring more."

Mother Johanna had a good heart and agreed. With her the two boys sewed small sacks out of the big ones and filled them with grain. The manager of the warehouse was not very happy when Johanna asked him for half of all the grain they had in storage, but he had to oblige.

From then on Nicholas and Pico were often seen with their cart bringing little sacks of corn to the poor people of the city. Pico knew where the need was greatest. Again and again the two boys approached houses at dusk. They liked leaving their gifts on windowsills or in front of the doors. After knocking on the doors they would run away before anyone saw them. Watching from a hiding place, they enjoyed the surprised looks on the faces of people when they found the gifts that had been left for them.

One day father Epiphanius returned from his sea journey. He brought new grain with him. He expected that through his sales his manager would have made a great deal of money. However, when Johanna told him how differently everything had developed and how busily the boys had worked in order to still the hunger in the poor part of the city, Epiphanius said: "In the Gospel it says: He who has two shirts, give one to him who has none." And he was satisfied.

Little Trips Around the Neighborhood

One day Nicholas and Pico were on their way home pulling their empty cart. In front of an apartment they met a girl whose legs were paralyzed. She sat by the street corner and played with a little piece of wood in the dust of the road. Her mother stood beside her.

Nicholas spoke to Pico: "Let's take her for a ride." Right away he stepped over to her mother and asked: "What is the name of your child? Can she not walk at all?" Surprised, the mother looked at the well-dressed Nicholas and answered: "Her name is Aspa. No, she cannot walk." Then Nicholas asked her: "May we take Aspa for a little ride and show her the city?" Aspa called out: "Yes, mother, how wonderful it would be to drive around!"

"But I will come along," said the mother. Aspa clapped her hands with excitement and did not mind at all when the bold boys lifted her into the carriage. It was a wonderful ride for Aspa. She laughed with delight. When they came through the city park they approached the pond, where there were ducks. Right beside the pond a lame boy was playing in the sand. His mother had carried him there in her arms. Right away the two boys placed him, too, into the carriage, and his mother followed along.

The next day there were already four children in the cart. When they went uphill Nicholas and Pico were quite

out of breath; they began to sweat and Nicholas had trouble breathing. One day, after he had had a particularly hard time with his breathing: he said: "I am going to ask Dad for a donkey. Then it will be easier. We will be able to take turns with our trips around the neighborhood."

In his father's storage area there were three donkeys that had to carry sacks of grain from one place to another. Again and again Nicholas was allowed to harness one of his gray friends. When the two boys traveled with their cart through the city people would often stop and say: "Look! There is Nicholas the good one and Pico the rascal." But after a year one could hear: "Look! Pico and Niko are coming." Everybody loved them.

In one way Pico was different from his friend. Niko loved to visit churches. With reverence he listened to the songs of the monks. He often visited them and learned to read and write from them. He also served during mass. Pico on the other hand liked to visit craftsmen. When he was older he was allowed to travel with Epiphanius. At first he was just a deck hand, but later he became a sailor. The two friends could only rarely meet, but each was happy with what life had to offer.

Nicholas Loses His Parents

A terrible illness broke out in the region where Nicholas and Pico lived and in a few days Nicholas' parents died from it. When they were buried, the trustworthy manager came to Nicholas and handed him his rich legacy. Nicholas asked the manager to carry on his father's business as he had already done for so many years.

Now Nicholas was able to help even more people. Whenever possible, he did so secretly. Meanwhile he had become a young priest in the town of Myra and was well known as a benefactor to many people. Everyone knew him as "the good Nicholas." Wherever possible he helped and served the people. His estate decreased but in his soul he grew richer.

Close by his house there lived a father who had three young daughters. Their mother had died after a long illness. All their savings had been used up and they had grown very poor. The girls would have loved to get married but at that time it was not possible to get married without some money for a dowry.

Nicholas heard about it. He looked for three money-bags, placed into each a few gold coins, and wrote a girl's name on each one of them, tying it on the pouch. One evening he went for a walk and found the window of their house open. He threw the three pouches into the room and disappeared quickly around the corner. Hearing the noise, the father and his three daughters hurried into the room.

17

18

Angrily the father demanded to know "who is throwing stones?" "Just come and see," called one of the daughters. On the floor were three valuable purses, each with the name of one of the girls and under the name it said, "Money for Marriage." The girls danced around the room. The father ran into the street. There was no one to be seen. They guessed who it was that had helped them and Nicholas was invited to a triple wedding. In this way Nicholas founded three happy families.

The Three Knights

Nicholas had become very well known in his city. When he gave his sermon on Sunday people of his city listened piously. It was not surprising that they came to him with all their worries.

One morning there was a knock on his door. It was still quite early. When Nicholas opened the door, he saw standing before him a very elegantly dressed lady. She was crying so hard that at first she could not speak to him at all. Nicholas invited her into the house. When she had sat down and become a little calmer, one word rapidly followed the other: "I have had news this morning that my husband and two of his friends are going to be executed just outside the city in the place of judgment. My husband is innocent and so are the other two. The judge could not find any fault with any of them; however, they have an enemy who bribed the judge with sums of money so that he would pronounce a guilty verdict and send them to their death. The prison warden sent me a secret letter during the night, which said that this morning was the day on which they would be executed. Nicholas, only you can help them! Come with me to the place of execution! Save them!"

"Let us leave immediately!" answered Nicholas. The two hurried to the place of execution.

When they arrived, they found that the henchmen had already blindfolded the men. The executioner in a red

gown stood ready with his sword. The knights were asked to kneel. Just at that moment Nicholas came running onto the scene. The woman was almost unable to keep up with him and arrived a little later. Nicholas was tall and strong. He charged the executioner, who fell backward and Nicholas managed to tear the sword away from him. Dumbfounded the man sat up. In a thundering voice Nicholas said: "We are not beheading anyone here. I will have to go and speak to the judge."

As Nicholas loosened the shackles around their limbs, he spoke to the knights: "Follow me immediately to the house of judgment." He threw some silver coins to the executioner and his helpers and left with the three knights. On the way they told him in detail what had happened. Now Nicholas had proof of their innocence. When they reached the judge's house, Nicholas asked the three knights to wait until he gave them a sign. A servant led him inside. He was announced to the judge and was asked to see him immediately.

In righteous anger Nicholas thundered at the keeper of the law and accused him of judging falsely in the case of the three knights. The judge listened unwillingly. When Nicholas forcefully pronounced the name of the donor who had bribed him he seemed momentarily shaken to the core. However, he quickly regained control, saying: "There is no need to get excited. The judgment has been made and fulfilled. The three knights are dead."

Nicholas went to the open window and shouted only two words: "Come up." Soon the three accused appeared in the room, silent and earnest. The judge became pale and suddenly began to rage: "I will allow the executioner to do his duty!"

Nicholas made a sign to the three knights to leave the room. When he was alone once again with the judge he said: "Sir, you have been given your position by his majesty the Emperor. If you do not make amends and deal with this situation in the proper way, I will speak to the Emperor myself. I will give you until tomorrow. You are going to use the bribes you accepted for the poor of the country and with this you will do penance. Once more you will receive the opportunity to carry on in your position as judge. Many people have spoken to me that your judgments are generally law-abiding and wise. Every human being makes mistakes at times. You too can be forgiven when you show that you are sorry." After these words Nicholas left the chamber.

Next day a messenger came to Nicholas with a sealed package. A large sum of gold was in it. A piece of parchment paper lay on top: "Forgive me, Nicholas, and pray for me!"

How Nicholas Became a Bishop

The time came when the Bishop of Myra passed away. A few bishops from around the country were therefore summoned to meet at the monastery near the large church. They had to meet to choose a new bishop for Myra. During the night before the meeting the head bishop had a dream. He heard a voice speaking to him: "Be on guard at midnight before the gate of the church. The first person who comes to the church is meant to be the new bishop."

In the evening the head bishop assembled all the others in a chapel of the city church. He revealed his dream to them and begged them not to leave the chapel but to remain praying silently until he came back. He himself was going to guard the entrance of the church. Within the dark church only one light was seen, that of the eternal flame.

Meanwhile Nicholas had received the parcel with the gold from the judge. His soul was so filled with gratitude that when he wanted to sleep at night, he found no rest. He decided to go to the church, although it was already midnight. He wanted to offer a prayer of gratitude before the altar for the successful saving of the three knights and the conversion of the judge.

He went on his way. Just as he was about to go through the church door, a figure approached him, coming from the darkness of the church. He asked him: "Who are

you?" "I am Nicholas, a low servant of the church. Why do you take my time? I just want to say an evening prayer in front of the altar."

The figure disappeared. Nicholas entered. In the middle of his prayer he was disturbed. The head bishop had gone to the chapel and called: "Brothers, he has come. His name is Nicholas. He is meant to become the new bishop. Take lights and come with me."

Nicholas could hardly believe his ears, when from the back of the church he heard a hymn to praise the Lord. A small procession of bishops, each holding a candle, moved solemnly towards the altar. Quickly he got on his feet and tried to hide behind a column. However, they had already seen him and encircled him with the lights. The hymn ended and the head bishop spoke: "Nicholas, the prophetic sign has been fulfilled. You are the new Bishop of Myra!" He was led by the arm to the empty bishop's chair in the choir section. When he tried to resist, the bishop in charge pressed him into the chair. Nicholas had to let it happen. They brought the red bishop's cloak and enveloped him in it.

On the following day one could hear voices in the city and in the countryside proclaiming the new bishop. "Myra has a new Bishop. His name is Nicholas." All the people were rejoicing because his name was so well known and he was loved by everyone. In spite of his increased work, he did not forget to go from time to time to the children and to the poor to bring them gifts with his donkey.

Often he took Pico with him as a servant, for he had returned from a life at sea. He served and cooked for the bishop. Sometimes he even took out the small old cart when they went jointly into the city; here and there you could see one two or three children sitting in it. They loved being driven around.

Famine

Once again the harvest was poor. Hunger had returned to the citizens of Myra. One day Nicholas received news of three ships filled to the brim with valuable grain. They had anchored in the harbor and were meant to proceed tomorrow to Constantinople to the Emperor. They remained in the harbor for only one night. People had tried to buy some grain, and, pleading for help, they had spoken about the famine that had hit Myra. But the master of the ship refused all who asked.

Immediately Nicholas went with Pico to the harbor to speak to the ships' owner. He was well received and someone was sent immediately to make him a gift of three sacks of grain for his own kitchen. Nicholas refused to accept the gift and the shipmaster said: "I do not have permission to sell any of this grain. This shipment is for the Emperor."

Nicholas described the dire situation in the city and reported that people had already died of hunger. He spoke directly to the conscience of the shipmaster: "Do you want to be responsible for the death of many hundreds of people? I will make the following proposal. Each of your ships has many hundred sacks of grain on board. From each ship give a hundred sacks to the city. In return I will be your prisoner. Take me on your ship as a guarantor and together we will go to Constantinople. I will speak to the Emperor and answer all of his questions. You will not be held responsible."

With a heavy heart the shipmaster agreed. Nicholas sent for Pico and said to him: "Remain in the city. Guard and distribute the grain in my name. Then the grain will be shared fairly." That was how Myra was saved from starvation.

Nicholas Sails to the Emperor

A terrible storm arose during the long sea voyage to the Emperor of Constantinople. If every one of the three ships had not unloaded a hundred sacks of grain in Myra, they would all have been lost to the high waves. When the storm was at its worst, Nicholas went up to the swaying deck. He held fast to the mast and shouted loud words into the wind. The sailors thought that he had commanded the wild wind to calm down, because soon afterwards the terrible roaring stopped and the waves lost their powerful impact on the ships.

After the arrival of the ships in the harbor of Constantinople, everybody left to go ashore. Nicholas went immediately to the Emperor's palace. A bishop was allowed to enter and speak to the Emperor, without delay. The Emperor began the conversation: "I have heard that you come from Myra. Why did you undertake that difficult journey across the sea?"

Nicholas replied: "Highest Emperor! I am in your debt. The people in my poor city of Myra had been starving for weeks. It is still many months before a new harvest can be counted on. I am the shepherd of my flock in Myra. Should I stand by and watch them die one by one? So I went to your ships—heavily laden with grain—that had anchored in our harbor on route from Egypt. I ordered the shipmaster to unload one hundred sacks from each ship for my hungry citizens. I then handed myself over as a prisoner to your shipmaster. I myself came to your majesty to account for my deed. During the second week at sea there was a frightful storm and the ships could possibly have sunk had not a hundred sacks of grain been taken off of each ship. You see, dear Emperor, you have rescued thousands from starvation and your ships have arrived safely in your harbor."

Emperor Constantine could become very angry when something happened against his wishes. His punishment could be terrible. But as he listened to Nicholas, whose heart spoke louder than his tongue, he remained calm. His head sank low as he was listening to the events that Nicholas described, so low that his crown almost fell from his head.

When he lifted his head again, he looked Nicholas squarely in the eye and said: "Nicholas, I believe every word you have said. You are not one to try and flatter me. I fully respect a man like you. I'll forgive you and give the grain as a gift to your city." Then he motioned Nicholas to come closer to him, gave him his hand, and invited him to dinner at the Emperor's table." While they were eating Nicholas sat next to the Emperor who said to him: "Nicholas, in six months there will be a large church council meeting in Nicaea. For this I hope to invite bishops from all over Christendom. Come back then. Your good, wise words must be heard." After dinner he presented Nicholas with a beautiful silver goblet for his church and sent him off with his blessings. When Nicholas returned to his city weeks later, the citizens greeted him with joy. Pico had started a few soup kitchens. Here all the poor could come to eat every day. Nobody was hungry any more.

Nicholas Goes to the Council of Nicaea

In accordance with the wishes of the Emperor, Nicholas traveled to Nicaea in the year 325 to attend the big gathering of bishops. This is called a church council. Several hundred bishops were invited to come to the Emperor to discuss the teachings of Christianity.

The meeting took place in the Emperor's palace. Nicholas listened; often the bishops spoke harshly to each other and sometimes they even quarreled. He remained silent. Towards the end of the council, the Emperor sent for him and said: "Nicholas, you have not spoken a single word all day. Before they all depart again, I would like to hear you speak to them. Tomorrow is the last day." Nicholas answered: "Highest Emperor, if the spirit moves me, I will speak."

On the following day Nicholas took the floor and began: "Highest Emperor, dear brothers in Christ! In Christianity every year we celebrate the baptism of Jesus Christ in the Jordan on the sixth of January. On that day God's Son, the Christ, coming from the heights of the heavens, united with the human being Jesus. This is and will remain a major festival. But in our Christian year we could also celebrate the day when the Jesus child was born on the earth. The Gospel of St. Luke speaks about a shepherd child, while St. Matthew tells us about a kingly child."

One of the bishops interrupted: "But the Gospels don't give us the date of His birth!"

Nicholas ignored the interruption and continued: "Light shone into the darkness, so I would like to suggest that in the future, Christians celebrate this earthly birth of the child during the darkest nights of the year, around the end of December." When Nicholas had finished speaking, a mumbling could be heard among the bishops. Some of them agreed, while others said: "Don't we have enough church festivals as things are?"

As the arguments grew louder, the Emperor stood up and demanded silence. He then said: "Take this beautiful thought from Bishop Nicholas from Myra with you. He who wants to celebrate the earthly birth of the child should do it from now on during the darkest days of the year."

That same year, around the end of December, in the church of Myra, Nicholas was one of the first to celebrate the Holy Nights. On one altar he placed the crèche with the shepherds, and on another he showed the visit of the kings from the Orient. Gradually other churches began to celebrate like this also. In this way the Christmas festival found its way into Christianity. Thus Nicholas became the herald of Christmas as we know it today.

How Nicholas Appeared in the Emperor's Dream

Among all the councilors in the Emperor's palace was one who was unfaithful. He had a grudge against three knights whom he felt were being favored by the Emperor. They were the knights who many years before had suffered the injustice in Myra from which Nicholas had saved them.

Out of envy the false advisor whispered to the Emperor: "Those three have said bad things about you. Before you they appear like white doves, but behind your back they creep like serpents and spread their poison against you." Then he told the Emperor an untrue story about them.

The Emperor could hardly contain his anger about the unfaithfulness of the three knights and without further investigation he had them put into a dungeon. When they were together in the dark they turned their thoughts to Nicholas and implored him to help them. Lo and behold, during that night Nicholas appeared to the Emperor in his dream saying: "The three knights are innocent. Let them go free!" Nicholas looked at him with such sad eyes that the Emperor awoke feeling quite disturbed.

The strange fact was that Nicholas also appeared in the false advisor's dream, telling him with thunderous words and fiery eyes that he should confess the truth.

35

In the morning when the advisor appeared before the Emperor, the Emperor said to him: "During the night Nicholas came to me, telling me to let the three knights go free because they are innocent." A pain shot through the councilor's legs. He sank to his knees and admitted right there and then his shameful deed. The Emperor had the three knights brought before him, and asked them: "What kind of magic do you hide that you can disturb my dreams? Do you know a person called Nicholas?" The three knights threw up their hands and told the story of how Nicholas had saved them from the executioner in Myra many years ago, and that in the previous night they had implored him to save them again because they were innocent. The Emperor saw the truth and spoke: "Thank God and his servant Nicholas! He has saved you a second time. Should you meet him again, ask him to pray for the Emperor and his kingdom. His prayers are strong." The false councilor fell into disfavor, and was forbidden to enter the Emperor's palace again.

The Thief's Candle

Near Myra there lived a man who was called Raffer. He was a joker and a vagabond. Every day he wandered around the houses and whenever he saw something lying around he took it with him. He carried a sack and the objects simply disappeared into it. As time went on he became more and more daring; he slipped into houses and stole china, laundry, jewelry, and anything else that could be crammed into his bag. Once the bag was full he would wander into another village or into the town of Myra itself and sell the things that he had stolen. He was so skillful at this that he could often sell the things for two or three times their value. When he had had a good day, and had counted his money, he used to go to church and thank God for his successful day's work. He thought nothing about it at all.

One day when he had stolen something in a village, he was caught, but was able to escape. He ran as fast as his feet would carry him. However, the owner called a neighbor and together they ran after him along the street to the outskirts of the village. Raffer had gained some distance on them but heaven help him if he should tire. While fleeing, he met an old man sitting on the wayside. Raffer stopped for a moment and called out: "Hey, old man, can you help me find a hiding place? I am being chased! I am afraid that they will kill me!" The old man replied: "Go a little further! Lie down in the ditch on the left along the street. There you will see a dead horse that was never buried. Hide yourself quite close to it." The thief did this, even though the horse stank terribly.

His pursuers drew near, carrying swords. While passing they shouted to the old man: "Did you see a man with a sack?" The old man pointed down the path and they ran on.

After a time Raffer got up from his hiding place and went to the old man to thank him: "Dear grandfather, I almost choked to death. It was such an awful smell!" The old man admonished: "You see, so do your thief's candles stink to heaven when you light them in the church." Raffer stood there as though struck by lightening. The old man wandered off and left him standing there. During the night Raffer took all the stolen goods back to the houses in the village. He burned his sack and began to look for honest work. He never stole again. To himself he thought: "This old man must have been Nicholas, who knows everything."

When Nicholas
Left the Earth

Just as all people have to think of leaving the earth some day, so Nicholas too had to think of his passing. Often he thought to himself: "Who will look after all the poor and the children when I am gone? Who will bring them gifts?" One day he had an idea. He invited Pico and some of his other friends to visit him. When they were all assembled, he began by saying: "My life is nearing its end. I know it. I am going into another life. But I still have one major earthly concern: Who in this city of Myra will give presents to the poor and to the children?"

Enthusiastically they all spoke at the same time: "We, your friends, will do this!" And Pico added: "Our little cart is old, but it still works. As long as I am able to I shall take it to the poor and to the children." Nicholas answered: "You may do it in my name; then you will be a true Nicholas, the Pico-Nicho!" All of the friends laughed happily.

Nicholas continued: "Everywhere in the world people should do this, not just in Myra. It is important to make one's brothers and sisters happy, to help the poor and the sick. He who does so in my name is himself a true Nicholas. He is a herald of the Christmas festival. I look back on my life with gratitude, because I was privileged to help many people." A few days later Nicholas was again visited by his friends. Suddenly without any warning, while he was talking to them, he felt weak. His head fell back on his chair. His eyes looked upwards. Slowly his life ebbed away and peacefully his soul departed from his body.

The passing of Bishop Nicholas was a surprise to his friends. For a while they remained silent, each one absorbed in prayer. One of the friends who was present at the time of his death later recalled that it was as though they heard a distant choir singing, and that the singing probably came from the realm of angels.

His friends placed his body on a bed and went out to buy candles. It was the evening of December 6th. The news spread like wildfire through the city: "Nicholas, the Good, has died." Every one wanted to come and say good-bye. His coffin was taken to the church. Someone had opened the lid so that one could see his kind loving face. Some of the people said: "He is still smiling." Others felt: "He looks at me sternly."

Because there were few flowers at that time of year, people brought hundreds of candles and little oil lamps. The entire church was a great sea of light. On the streets there were groups of people everywhere. They talked about Nicholas and told stories of what they had experienced with him. After three days his body was placed into a sarcophagus made of stone. On it someone placed a placard on which could be read the words:

NICHOLAS
FRIEND OF CHILDREN - HELPER OF THE POOR
PROTECTOR OF THE PERSECUTED
SAVIOR FROM STORMS

From then on there was not a day in the year when people did not come to bring a light to his tomb. The church was called Nicholas Church. For one could see that he had truly led a pious life. From then on, he was called St. Nicholas. The news of his life and work was slowly spread into all Christian countries.

On December 6th, on his day of death, the poor in the city of Myra were allowed to go to the houses of the rich, where presents were given to them in the name of Nicholas. The friends who had been asked by Nicholas to come to his place before his death founded a Nicholas Brotherhood. Whenever possible they traveled about, doing good in his name. But he who wishes to be Nicholas on the 6th of December should think of him and then he will be a true Nicholas.

The Innocent Servant

The rich old merchant Timotheus walked through the rows of slaves offered as servants in the slave market in Constantinople. Among all the dull lifeless faces he noticed an intelligent youth with sad eyes. He approached him and asked his name. The youth answered: "My name is Marius. I am from the city Myra." The merchant asked him: "What can you do? Have you ever served at table?" Marius answered: "Yes, my good master died. I served him all his meals." Timotheus responded: "Ah, that is how you came to the market. Are you a Christian?" "Yes, my name tells me so. I never knew my parents, but they had me baptized."

The merchant went to the slave trader and began to bargain with him for the slave Marius. They agreed on a price. The merchant paid some gold coins and asked Marius to follow him. When they reached a large house, Marius noticed several other slave-servants. However, he was being trained as his master's personal servant and to serve his master at the table. He had to run errands, polish his shoes, and sometimes go with him into the city. The old gentleman was somewhat forgetful and often could not find the place in the city to which he wanted to go so he valued Marius's service and was good to him.

One day a man who had bought a house from Timotheus came to the house. The visitor had brought him the total payment in gold pieces. When the money was counted and the dealings had come to an end,

Timotheus rang the bell so that Marius could take the visitor to the door. Marius entered the room and saw the shining gold pieces on the table. He took the stranger along the corridor and down the stairs and said good-bye with three low bows.

Merchant Timotheus wiped the gold pieces he had received and put them into a large leather pouch. He then placed the pouch into a wooden box. Soon he took it out of the box and placed it under the mattress of his bed. A little later he took the pouch away again and hid it in a stone oven that was not heated during the summer. Soon after, Marius entered the room. He had come to prepare a footbath for his master.

The next day the master had totally forgotten that he had placed the money in the oven. He tore off the doors and lids of all his wooden boxes and searched for his money. Suddenly he also dragged the mattress from the bed. Where was the pouch of gold coins? He couldn't find it! In his excitement he sounded the gong, which was a sign for Marius to come and see him.

When Marius entered, the old merchant screamed at him: "Have you seen the brown leather pouch? Did you take it away?" "No, Sir," Marius responded, "but I will help you search for it!" The master followed him wherever the servant searched for it. Suddenly he screamed: "You were the only one who saw the beautiful gold. You must have stolen it. Where did you hide it?"

Marius tried everything to convince his master that he was innocent. But in his master's eyes he was a thief.

Timotheus called for the doorkeeper and a servant from the courtyard and told them that Marius had stolen a leather pouch full of money. "Take him! Lead him into the cellar and whip him until he confesses where he has hidden the money." Roughly they carried the innocent Marius down the steps, tore his clothes off, and tied him to a post. With a leather whip they beat him mercilessly. Again and again Marius cried in his pain: "I have not taken the money!" Finally he became unconscious and was silent. Blood ran down his whole body.

The doorkeeper went to the master upstairs, shook his shoulder, and said: "I cannot do a thing! He denies having taken it. We kept beating him until he became unconscious." In bitterness and anger the merchant spoke: "Never did I think he would do such a thing! He was such a good chap. Leave him hang tied to the post overnight! He will admit to his dreadful deed tomorrow morning." Hours later that night, Marius woke up from his unconscious state. His whole body burned from the wounds. In his despair he began to beg and implore Nicholas: "Oh, Nicholas, you are the father of righteousness, please help me! You know that I am innocent!" It was for him as though there appeared a shimmer of light in the deep darkness. His exhausted, maltreated body fell asleep.

At the same time Timotheus, sleeping upstairs, had a dream. Nicholas appeared to him and said: "Your gold is in the oven. Why do you bring such suffering to the poor boy?"

The merchant woke up, sat up in bed, and stared for a moment into the oil lamp, which burned next to his bedside. Then he got out of bed, took the lamp to the oven, and opened the little door. Behind it lay his gold! The oil lamp was shaking in his hand as he sat down on the oven bench and stared in front of him. Then he got up, slipped into his coat, and took the little lamp with him as he descended into the cellar.

When the heavy door creaked open, Marius woke up, lifted his head, and sighed. Timotheus looked aghast at the young man. Blood covered his whole body. He took a couple of steps towards him and placed the oil light on the floor.

Timotheus laid his shaking hand on top of Marius's head. He whispered: "Marius !" The servant lifted his face and noticed that Timotheus was pulling a shining knife from his belt. In his dulled state of mind, Marius thought: "Now if he kills me I will go to Nicholas. He knows everything." Not a muscle moved in his body when the knife cut. He felt no pain, only heard a dull thump. Timotheus had cut the rope with which he was tied. Marius fell to the floor and lay there. Timotheus could hardly walk he was so shaken. He was looking for the doorkeeper.

When Marius came to himself, it was dawn. He was lying in a bed. Next to him sat Timotheus, still holding the oil lamp in his hand. Marius turned his face towards him. He was unable to speak. But now Timotheus spoke to him: "Marius, you are innocent. Forgive me! I have found the gold. Nicholas..."

He could say no more. Marius noticed how Timotheus cried. Slowly he stretched his wounded hand towards him. It fell onto Timotheus' knee. The old man bent over and touched it gently. The morning light began to shine through the window. Timotheus went to get a female servant to put healing herbs on his wounds.

When, after several days, Marius had almost recovered and Timotheus was again sitting by him, he said: "Marius, you shall no longer be a slave! I give you your freedom. And I give you all the gold. It has brought enough misfortune to us both. But now it shall make you happy."

The Knights of Bari

Over the centuries many churches and chapels were built on the Mediterranean coast in Nicholas' name. When the Turks entered the land and conquered Asia Minor, the city of Myra also fell to them and was placed under the flag of the half moon. During these wars, the church of Nicholas caught fire and now lay in ruins. Most of the Christians fled on ships across the sea to Greece, Italy, and Sicily.

A number of knights had ended up in the city of Bari. Once when they were sitting together and thinking back to their lost land and beloved city of Myra, one of the knights spoke: "It pains me that Nicholas' grave has been lost and that his blessed remains now lie in a heathen country. Could we not attempt to bring them here? We could try to find his burial site. When our ship carrying merchandise enters the harbor, it could be docked and we could go during the night to the destroyed church of Nicholas. We will surely be able to find the actual grave. His remains should be brought to Bari and put to a rest worthy of Nicholas. The church should then be called Nicholas' Church.

When the knight had finished talking, all the other knights were very excited. It was a great idea. One of them called out: "We will take weapons. We will surprise them! If we are a few dozen, we can gain entry by force. We shall simply do away with any who step in our way." An older knight spoke: "Should we sacrifice human blood for the sake of Nicholas' bones? What would he himself say if we were to act in such a way? No, under no circumstances may we desecrate his remains by shedding human blood."

The knights became quiet. Finally one of them asked to speak: "Friends," he said, "we will travel there and place our destiny into Nicholas' hand. If it is meant to be he will assist us." All heeded this advice. A week later a trading-ship sailed from Bari, heading in the direction of Myra. It was laden with building materials. The knights thought: "Wood is needed in every city. We will surely be given permission to drop anchor in the harbor. We will sell the planks and boards to the city. At the same time we will bring our adventure to its desired conclusion."

A favorable wind enabled the ship to reach the harbor in Myra after a trip of only three weeks. The forty-seven knights had disguised themselves as sailors and carpenters. But just in case, they carried sharp daggers under their clothing.

When the ship had anchored, the harbor police approached them in a dinghy. They used a rope ladder to climb on board. The Turks were armed with scimitars. More than half the knights hid below deck behind the wood stored in the bowels of the ship. They did not want to arouse any suspicion. Through an interpreter the police captain asked: "What kind of goods do you have to offer as you have obviously come to anchor in our harbor to trade. Until now no Christian ships have docked here." The shipmaster from Bari answered: "We have wood to build with, and we sell it for good silver." The police captain answered: "The city can make good use of it. Come with me to the city's purchasing agent and take along two of your companions. We will find out whether there is any interest in buying your wood." The shipmaster took two of his friends who knew the city of Myra and Nicholas' church very well. With their own boat they followed the Turks to the shore. Two knights were charged with keeping watch until their return. The road to the city's treasurer led past the destroyed Nicholas church, where charred timbers stood out desolately. Only the back part of the church was still intact. It was there that Nicholas' grave was situated. One could still find part of the roof leaning on one of the walls of the church. This part of the town was almost uninhabited, because so much had been destroyed.

The treasurer was willing to buy the wood, and said: "Tomorrow morning I will come to your ship. I would like to look at the quality of the wood, and decide whether measure and price are right for our purposes." The Turkish captain spoke to his interpreter: "Take the strangers back to the harbor, but don't let them out of your sight! I have some business to attend to in town." The three knights began to return to their ship. When they were close to the Nicholas church, the shipmaster gave a silver coin to the interpreter saying: "We would enjoy a little walk around the city, and we will be able to find our way back to the ship by ourselves. You can go home." The interpreter replied: "I may not leave you for a second until we arrive back at the harbor. After all, you might be spies."

Then the shipmaster had a brilliant idea that hit him like lightening. He turned to the interpreter: "We still need to look for a good place to store the wood until it is to be used. We must find a place where it will be protected from the rain. Over there, close to the tall building, I can see a sound piece of roof. Let us have a look at that roof!"

The interpreter had nothing against this. The knights stepped into the ruined church, the church in which Nicholas had preached to his people. Church hymns and prayers had once filled the air. They were moved to tears. Then they came to the place where Nicholas' grave was. The memorial plaque was nowhere to be seen. It had been covered in dust and dirt. The knights whispered to each other: "It is going to work!"

The shipmaster said to the interpreter: "This would not be a suitable place for the long planks." Then they slowly walked back to the harbor. Early next morning the city treasurer appeared with a few builders. They boarded the ship, looked at the sizes of some of the planks, and were satisfied. Because the knights offered a good price they soon reached an agreement.

The administrator was especially pleased when the strangers offered the services of their sailors to transport the wood into town in order to find a suitable place to store it. He immediately paid the sum that had been agreed upon, but he did leave a few men of the harbor police aboard the ship until the wood had been brought to land.

He ordered a smaller boat to pull up along side in order to take the wood to the shore. The harbor police could hardly believe the number of sailors that suddenly appeared from nowhere! They felt that something was not right, but then they saw how efficiently the sailors worked. They indeed behaved as if work were their greatest joy.

Underneath the planks a wooden box was hidden. Two of the sailors carried it carefully to the small boat and then to the shore. In it were tools, hammers, chisels, shovels, and a linen cloth. It looked like a small wooden coffin and they did not open it until they arrived at the ruins of the Nicholas church.

The supervisor appointed by the town's administrator watched as the planks were placed next to the pile of broken stones. However it was such a noisy and dusty process that he stayed somewhat to the side of it all. Now they began to use their shovels to clean a place for the wood, and soon there appeared the stone plate.

NICHOLAS
FRIEND OF CHILDREN - HELPER OF THE POOR
PROTECTOR OF THE PERSECUTED
SAVIOR FROM STORMS

Because the sailors shoveled with so much noise, throwing the planks down and rolling them over, others were able to loosen the gravestone and open it without being noticed. Without any problems the bones of Nicholas soon came into view. He was a person who had done so much good on the earth. The knights laid the earthly remains of Nicholas onto the linen that they had brought with them and placed them carefully into the wooden coffin. They laid their hammers, chisels, and shovels on top and then tipped the stone back down onto the empty grave. Unfortunately it was too heavy to take along.

But in a corner they also discovered a broken portion of a small column of red stone lying in the ruins of the church. A strong knight said: "This one we will take as a memento of the first Nicholas church." Immediately others were engaged in placing ropes around it and six of the men were able to lift the column in order to bring it to the ship.

52

When the knights had finished their task and were about to take the wooden box back to their ship, the interpreter said: "A box made from planks is also wood, and therefore belongs to the city. Leave it right here!" The shipmaster surprised the interpreter by opening the lid of the box, saying: "These are our tools. Our workbox is coming with us!" "What do you want to do with that piece of stone?" The captain asked through the interpreter? The master of the ship answered: "This we will take with us as a souvenir of the city Myra in which long ago the good Nicholas lived." "Unknown to us," said the interpreter, "we only know of the prophet Mohammed."

On this day many people had come to the shore and had observed the transaction. When the last knight had gone aboard, the anchor was lifted and a flag with a cross was pulled up on the mast. The Turkish people heard with astonishment and wonder how forty-seven knights sang a hymn of gratitude with all their might. Of course it was meant as a celebration because they had succeeded in their task of saving the earthly remains of Nicholas.

A light wind moved the sails and white seagulls accompanied the ship. Slowly it disappeared into the blue horizon. After a safe journey the ship finally arrived in Bari, and the good news spread like wildfire: "The ship with Nicholas has arrived! Be joyful Bari! Let all the bells of the city sound!" The joy was so great that the people very soon afterwards set about building a Saint-Nicholas-Church. His remains finally had a worthy resting place and all his friends had a sanctuary for prayer.

This church in Bari is now about one thousand years old. If you climb down into the crypt below the choir you can find the grave of Nicholas, radiant with the reflection of the many, many candles people have lit there. In a corner you can see the red column that the knights took with them. It is about as tall as a human being. It became necessary to erect a strong iron gate around it. Why? Because visitors started bringing knives to scrape off some dust from the column; this dust was mixed with water and drunk in hopes of its healing various illnesses. This is why deep furrows were scratched into the column. These furrows show the great love and trust that the people of Bari have for good Saint Nicholas. This love for him has never changed to this very day.